CROCK POT COOKBOOK FOR ONE

30 Easy delicious recipes for Every Slow Cooking Meal

Vivian Greene

COPYRIGHT © BY VIVIAN GREENE 2023.

All rights reserved.

Before this document is duplicated or reproduced in any manner, the publisher's consent must be gained. Therefore, the contents within can neither be stored electronically, transferred, nor kept in a database. Neither in Part nor full can the document be copied, scanned, faxed, or retained without approval from the publisher or creator

TABLE OF CONTENTS

Introduction 5

30 delicious crockpot recipes for busy beginners 7

    Pulled Pork Tacos: 7

    Beef Stew: 8

    Chicken Curry: 9

    Vegetable Soup: 10

    BBQ Chicken Wings: 11

    Moroccan Lamb Stew: 12

    Chili Con Carne: 13

    Teriyaki Chicken: 15

    Creamy Mushroom Soup: 17

    Beef and Broccoli: 18

    Lemon Garlic Chicken: 20

    Creamy Tuscan Chicken: 21

    Salsa Verde Chicken: 22

    Honey Garlic Meatballs: 23

    Buffalo Chicken Dip: 24

    Creamy Italian Chicken: 25

    Creamy Spinach Artichoke Dip: 26

Beef Bourguignon: 28
Hawaiian Pulled Chicken: 29
Tuscan White Bean Soup: 30
Teriyaki Pork Tenderloin: 32
Sweet and Spicy Barbecue Ribs: 33
Creamy Mushroom Risotto: 35
Thai Peanut Chicken: 36
Creamy Tomato Basil Soup 38
Beef Stroganoff 39
Vegetarian Chili: 40
Lemon Garlic Chicken: 42
Mexican Quinoa: 43
Chocolate Lava Cake: 44
Conclusion 46

INTRODUCTION

In a quaint town, bustling with the everyday rhythms of life, resided Emma, a young woman with a hectic schedule. Balancing her demanding job and personal commitments left her little time to prepare wholesome meals. However, a life-changing discovery awaited her in the form of a crockpot.

Emma welcomed a sleek crockpot into her kitchen, an appliance that would soon revolutionize her cooking experience. Each morning, she would gather fresh ingredients, effortlessly placing them into the crockpot before dashing off to work, setting the timer with a flick of her wrist.

Upon returning home, tantalizing aromas wafted through the air, leading her to the kitchen. As she lifted the lid, she was greeted by a symphony of perfectly cooked flavors. The crockpot had worked its magic, infusing the ingredients with rich tastes and textures.

Emma relished the benefits that the crockpot offered. Time-saving convenience allowed her to savor moments beyond the kitchen, while the crockpot's energy efficiency translated into reduced utility bills. Above all, she indulged in nutritious meals, as the slow cooking process preserved vital nutrients and intensified flavors.

With the crockpot as her culinary ally, Emma discovered newfound joy in cooking, relishing the effortless creation of mouthwatering dishes that nourished both her body and soul.

Cooking with a crockpot is a culinary miracle that combines flavor, convenience, and nutritious food. It is fundamentally the slow-and-gentle cooking method. With its low and constant heat, the crockpot gradually turns uncooked materials into mouthwatering culinary creations. It's a technique that needs little work yet provides enormous delight. The magic is in the way tastes combine, amplify, and evolve into complex symphonies of flavor. Using a crockpot, busy people may easily prepare filling meals that can warm their hearts and bodies. It's a celebration of simplicity that allows one to enjoy the benefits of delicious home cooking without having to stay in the kitchen.

30 DELICIOUS CROCKPOT RECIPES FOR BUSY BEGINNERS

Pulled Pork Tacos:

Ingredients:

1. 2 lbs pork shoulder
2. 1 cup barbecue sauce
3. 1/4 cup brown sugar
4. 2 tsp smoked paprika
5. 1 tsp garlic powder
6. Salt and pepper to taste

Instructions:

1. Place pork shoulder in the crockpot.
2. In a bowl, mix barbecue sauce, brown sugar, smoked paprika, garlic powder, salt, and pepper.

3. Pour the sauce over the pork shoulder, ensuring it's fully coated.
4. Cook on low for 8-10 hours or on high for 4-6 hours, until pork is tender and easily shreddable.
5. Shred the pork using two forks.
6. Serve in warm tortillas with your favorite toppings.

Prep Time: 15 minutes

Beef Stew:

Ingredients:

1. 2 lbs beef stew meat, cubed
2. 4 carrots, sliced
3. 3 potatoes, cubed
4. 1 onion, diced
5. 2 cloves garlic, minced
6. 4 cups beef broth
7. 1 cup red wine (optional)
8. 2 tbsp tomato paste
9. 2 tsp dried thyme
10. Salt and pepper to taste

Instructions:

1. Place beef, carrots, potatoes, onion, and garlic in the crockpot.
2. In a separate bowl, whisk together beef broth, red wine, tomato paste, thyme, salt, and pepper.
3. Pour the mixture over the ingredients in the crockpot.
4. Cook on low for 6-8 hours or on high for 3-4 hours, until meat is tender.
5. Adjust seasoning if needed.
6. Serve hot with crusty bread.

Prep Time: 20 minutes

Chicken Curry:

Ingredients:

1. 4 chicken breasts, boneless and skinless, cut into chunks
2. 1 onion, sliced
3. 2 cloves garlic, minced
4. 1 can coconut milk
5. 3 tbsp curry powder
6. 1 tbsp garam masala
7. 1 tsp turmeric
8. 1 tsp cumin
9. Salt and pepper to taste

10. Fresh cilantro, chopped (for garnish)

Instructions:

1. Place chicken, onion, and garlic in the crockpot.
2. In a bowl, mix together coconut milk, curry powder, garam masala, turmeric, cumin, salt, and pepper.
3. Pour the mixture over the chicken and stir to combine.
4. Cook on low for 4-6 hours or on high for 2-3 hours, until chicken is cooked through.
5. Serve over rice, garnished with fresh cilantro.

Prep Time: 15 minutes

Vegetable Soup:

Ingredients:

1. 4 cups vegetable broth
2. 2 cups diced tomatoes
3. 2 carrots, sliced
4. 2 stalks celery, diced
5. 1 onion, diced
6. 1 zucchini, diced

7. 1 cup green beans, chopped
8. 1 cup corn kernels
9. 1 tsp dried thyme
10. 1 tsp dried oregano
11. Salt and pepper to taste

Instructions:

1. Combine all ingredients in the crockpot.
2. Stir well to mix the flavors.
3. Cook on low for 6-8 hours or on high for 3-4 hours, until vegetables are tender.
4. Adjust seasoning if needed.
5. Serve hot with crusty bread.

Prep Time: 15 minutes

BBQ Chicken Wings:

Ingredients:

1. 2 lbs chicken wings
2. 1 cup barbecue sauce
3. 2 tbsp honey
4. 2 tbsp soy sauce
5. 2 cloves garlic, minced
6. 1 tsp paprika

7. Salt and pepper to taste
8. Chopped green onions (for garnish)

Instructions:

1. Place chicken wings in the crockpot.
2. In a bowl, mix together barbecue sauce, honey, soy sauce, garlic, paprika, salt, and pepper.
3. Pour the sauce over the chicken wings, making sure they are evenly coated.
4. Cook on low for 4-6 hours or on high for 2-3 hours, until chicken is cooked through.
5. Preheat the oven to broil.
6. Transfer the chicken wings to a baking sheet and broil for 5-7 minutes, until crispy.
7. Garnish with chopped green onions.

Prep Time: 10 minutes

Moroccan Lamb Stew:

Ingredients:

1. 2 lbs lamb stew meat, cubed
2. 1 onion, diced
3. 3 carrots, sliced
4. 2 cloves garlic, minced
5. 1 can diced tomatoes
6. 1 cup chicken broth
7. 2 tsp ground cumin
8. 1 tsp ground coriander
9. 1 tsp ground cinnamon
10. Salt and pepper to taste
11. Fresh cilantro, chopped (for garnish)

Instructions:

1. Place lamb, onion, carrots, garlic, diced tomatoes, chicken broth, cumin, coriander, cinnamon, salt, and pepper in the crockpot.
2. Stir well to combine the ingredients.
3. Cook on low for 6-8 hours or on high for 3-4 hours, until lamb is tender.
4. Adjust seasoning if needed.
5. Serve hot, garnished with fresh cilantro.

Prep Time: 20 minutes

Chili Con Carne:

Ingredients:

1. 1 lb ground beef
2. 1 onion, diced
3. 2 cloves garlic, minced
4. 1 can kidney beans, drained and rinsed
5. 1 can diced tomatoes
6. 1 cup beef broth
7. 2 tbsp chili powder
8. 1 tsp cumin
9. 1 tsp paprika
10. Salt and pepper to taste
11. Shredded cheese, sour cream, and sliced green onions (for garnish)

Instructions:

1. Brown ground beef in a skillet over medium heat until fully cooked. Drain excess fat.
2. Transfer the cooked beef, onion, garlic, kidney beans, diced tomatoes, beef broth, chili powder, cumin, paprika, salt, and pepper to the crockpot.
3. Stir well to combine.
4. Cook on low for 6-8 hours or on high for 3-4 hours, allowing the flavors to meld together.
5. Adjust seasoning if needed.

6. Serve hot, garnished with shredded cheese, sour cream, and sliced green onions.

Prep Time: 15 minutes

Teriyaki Chicken:

Ingredients:

1. 4 boneless, skinless chicken breasts
2. 1/2 cup soy sauce
3. 1/4 cup honey
4. 2 tbsp rice vinegar
5. 2 tbsp hoisin sauce
6. 2 cloves garlic, minced
7. 1 tsp ginger, grated
8. 1 tbsp cornstarch (optional, for thickening sauce)
9. Sesame seeds and sliced green onions (for garnish)

Instructions:

1. Place chicken breasts in the crockpot.

2. In a bowl, whisk together soy sauce, honey, rice vinegar, hoisin sauce, garlic, and ginger.
3. Pour the sauce over the chicken, ensuring it's evenly coated.
4. Cook on low for 4-6 hours or on high for 2-3 hours, until chicken is cooked through.
5. Optional: Remove the chicken from the crockpot and mix cornstarch with a little water. Stir the cornstarch mixture into the sauce in the crockpot to thicken it.
6. Serve the chicken over rice, garnished with sesame seeds and sliced green onions.

Prep Time: 10 minutes

Creamy Mushroom Soup:

Ingredients:

1. 1 lb mushrooms, sliced
2. 1 onion, diced
3. 3 cloves garlic, minced
4. 4 cups vegetable broth
5. 1 cup heavy cream
6. 2 tbsp flour
7. 2 tbsp butter
8. 1 tsp dried thyme
9. Salt and pepper to taste
10. Fresh parsley, chopped (for garnish)

Instructions:

1. Melt butter in a skillet over medium heat. Add mushrooms, onion, and garlic. Sauté until mushrooms are golden and onions are translucent.
2. Transfer the sautéed mixture to the crockpot.
3. Add vegetable broth and dried thyme. Stir well to combine.
4. Cook on low for 6-8 hours or on high for 3-4 hours, allowing the flavors to meld together.

5. In a small bowl, whisk together heavy cream and flour until smooth. Stir the mixture into the soup in the crockpot.
6. Cook for an additional 30 minutes, until the soup thickens slightly.
7. Adjust seasoning if needed.
8. Serve hot, garnished with fresh parsley.

Prep Time: 15 minutes

Beef and Broccoli:

Ingredients:

1. 1.5 lbs beef sirloin, thinly sliced
2. 4 cups broccoli florets
3. 1/2 cup low-sodium soy sauce
4. 1/4 cup hoisin sauce
5. 2 cloves garlic, minced
6. 2 tbsp cornstarch
7. 2 tbsp water
8. 2 tbsp sesame oil
9. Sesame seeds (for garnish)

Instructions:

1. Place beef and broccoli in the crockpot.
2. In a bowl, whisk together soy sauce, hoisin sauce, and garlic.
3. Pour the sauce over the beef and broccoli, ensuring they are coated.
4. Cook on low for 4-6 hours or on high for 2-3 hours, until beef is cooked through and broccoli is tender.
5. In a small bowl, mix cornstarch and water until smooth. Stir the mixture into the crockpot to thicken the sauce.
6. Drizzle sesame oil over the beef and broccoli before serving.
7. Garnish with sesame seeds.

Prep Time: 10 minutes

Lemon Garlic Chicken:

1. Ingredients:
2. 4 boneless, skinless chicken breasts
3. 1/4 cup lemon juice
4. 4 cloves garlic, minced
5. 2 tbsp olive oil
6. 1 tsp dried thyme
7. 1/2 tsp dried rosemary
8. Salt and pepper to taste
9. Fresh parsley, chopped (for garnish)

Instructions:

1. Place chicken breasts in the crockpot.
2. In a bowl, whisk together lemon juice, minced garlic, olive oil, dried thyme, dried rosemary, salt, and pepper.
3. Pour the mixture over the chicken, ensuring it's evenly coated.
4. Cook on low for 4-6 hours or on high for 2-3 hours, until chicken is cooked through.
5. Serve hot, garnished with fresh parsley.

Prep Time: 10 minutes

Creamy Tuscan Chicken:

Ingredients:

1. 4 boneless, skinless chicken breasts
2. 1 cup sun-dried tomatoes, chopped
3. 1 onion, sliced
4. 4 cloves garlic, minced
5. 1 cup chicken broth
6. 1 cup heavy cream
7. 2 cups spinach
8. 1 tsp dried oregano
9. Salt and pepper to taste
10. Grated Parmesan cheese (for garnish)

Instructions:

1. Place chicken breasts in the crockpot.
2. Add sun-dried tomatoes, onion, garlic, chicken broth, heavy cream, dried oregano, salt, and pepper.
3. Cook on low for 4-6 hours or on high for 2-3 hours, until chicken is cooked through.
4. Add spinach to the crockpot and stir until wilted.
5. Adjust seasoning if needed.
6. Serve hot, garnished with grated Parmesan cheese.

Prep Time: 10 minutes

Salsa Verde Chicken:

Ingredients:

1. 4 boneless, skinless chicken breasts
2. 1 jar (16 oz) salsa verde
3. 1 onion, sliced
4. 2 cloves garlic, minced
5. 1 tsp ground cumin
6. 1 tsp dried oregano
7. Salt and pepper to taste
8. Fresh cilantro, chopped (for garnish)

Instructions:

1. Place chicken breasts in the crockpot.
2. Add salsa verde, onion, garlic, ground cumin, dried oregano, salt, and pepper.
3. Cook on low for 4-6 hours or on high for 2-3 hours, until chicken is cooked through.
4. Shred the chicken using two forks.
5. Adjust seasoning if needed.
6. Serve hot, garnished with fresh cilantro.

Prep Time: 10 minutes

Honey Garlic Meatballs:

Ingredients:

1. 1.5 lbs ground beef
2. 1/2 cup breadcrumbs
3. 2 eggs
4. 1/4 cup honey
5. 1/4 cup soy sauce
6. 4 cloves garlic, minced
7. 1/4 tsp red pepper flakes (optional)
8. Chopped green onions (for garnish)

Instructions:

1. In a bowl, combine ground beef, breadcrumbs, eggs, and a pinch of salt and pepper. Mix well.
2. Shape the mixture into meatballs and place them in the crockpot.
3. In a separate bowl, whisk together honey, soy sauce, minced garlic, and red pepper flakes.
4. Pour the sauce over the meatballs, ensuring they are coated.

5. Cook on low for 4-6 hours or on high for 2-3 hours, until meatballs are cooked through.
6. Serve hot, garnished with chopped green onions.

Prep Time: 15 minutes

Buffalo Chicken Dip:

Ingredients:

1. 2 cups cooked chicken, shredded
2. 1 cup cream cheese
3. 1/2 cup buffalo sauce
4. 1/2 cup ranch dressing
5. 1/2 cup shredded cheddar cheese
6. 1/4 cup crumbled blue cheese (optional)
7. Chopped green onions (for garnish)

Instructions:

1. In the crockpot, combine cooked chicken, cream cheese, buffalo sauce, ranch dressing, shredded cheddar cheese, and crumbled blue cheese (if using).
2. Stir well to combine the ingredients.

3. Cook on low for 2-3 hours, until the dip is heated through and the cheese is melted.
4. Stir again to ensure all the ingredients are mixed.
5. Serve hot, garnished with chopped green onions.
6. Serve with tortilla chips or celery sticks.

Prep Time: 10 minutes

Creamy Italian Chicken:

Ingredients:

1. 4 boneless, skinless chicken breasts
2. 1 can condensed cream of chicken soup
3. 1/2 cup chicken broth
4. 1/2 cup sun-dried tomatoes, chopped
5. 2 cloves garlic, minced
6. 1 tsp dried basil
7. 1/2 tsp dried thyme
8. Salt and pepper to taste
9. Fresh basil leaves (for garnish)

Instructions:

1. Place chicken breasts in the crockpot.
2. In a bowl, whisk together cream of chicken soup, chicken broth, sun-dried tomatoes, minced garlic, dried basil, dried thyme, salt, and pepper.
3. Pour the mixture over the chicken, ensuring it's evenly coated.
4. Cook on low for 4-6 hours or on high for 2-3 hours, until chicken is cooked through.
5. Serve hot, garnished with fresh basil leaves.

Prep Time: 10 minutes

Creamy Spinach Artichoke Dip:

Ingredients:

1. 1 cup frozen chopped spinach, thawed and drained
2. 1 can artichoke hearts, drained and chopped
3. 1 cup cream cheese
4. 1/2 cup mayonnaise

5. 1/2 cup sour cream
6. 1/2 cup grated Parmesan cheese
7. 2 cloves garlic, minced
8. Salt and pepper to taste
9. Shredded mozzarella cheese (for garnish)
10. Chopped parsley (for garnish)

Instructions:

1. In the crockpot, combine spinach, artichoke hearts, cream cheese, mayonnaise, sour cream, Parmesan cheese, minced garlic, salt, and pepper.
2. Stir well to combine the ingredients.
3. Cook on low for 2-3 hours, until the dip is heated through and the cheeses are melted.
4. Stir again to ensure all the ingredients are mixed.
5. Sprinkle shredded mozzarella cheese over the top.
6. Cook for an additional 10-15 minutes, until the cheese is melted and bubbly.
7. Serve hot, garnished with chopped parsley.
8. Serve with tortilla chips or bread slices.

Prep Time: 10 minutes

Beef Bourguignon:

Ingredients:

1. 2 lbs beef chuck roast, cut into cubes
2. 1 onion, diced
3. 3 carrots, sliced
4. 3 cloves garlic, minced
5. 2 cups red wine
6. 1 cup beef broth
7. 2 tbsp tomato paste
8. 1 tsp dried thyme
9. 1 tsp dried rosemary
10. Salt and pepper to taste
11. Fresh parsley, chopped (for garnish)

Instructions:

1. Place beef, onion, carrots, and garlic in the crockpot.
2. In a separate bowl, whisk together red wine, beef broth, tomato paste, dried thyme, dried rosemary, salt, and pepper.
3. Pour the mixture over the ingredients in the crockpot.

4. Cook on low for 6-8 hours or on high for 3-4 hours, until beef is tender.
5. Adjust seasoning if needed.
6. Serve hot, garnished with fresh parsley.
7. Serve with crusty bread or mashed potatoes.

Prep Time: 20 minutes

Hawaiian Pulled Chicken:

Ingredients:

1. 4 boneless, skinless chicken breasts
2. 1 cup pineapple juice
3. 1/2 cup ketchup
4. 1/4 cup brown sugar
5. 1/4 cup soy sauce
6. 2 tbsp apple cider vinegar
7. 1 tsp garlic powder
8. Salt and pepper to taste
9. Pineapple slices (for garnish)
10. Fresh cilantro, chopped (for garnish)

Instructions:

1. Place chicken breasts in the crockpot.
2. In a bowl, whisk together pineapple juice, ketchup, brown sugar, soy sauce, apple cider vinegar, garlic powder, salt, and pepper.
3. Pour the mixture over the chicken, ensuring it's evenly coated.
4. Cook on low for 4-6 hours or on high for 2-3 hours, until chicken is cooked through.
5. Shred the chicken using two forks.
6. Adjust seasoning if needed.
7. Serve hot, garnished with pineapple slices and chopped cilantro.
8. Serve on hamburger buns or with rice.

Prep Time: 10 minutes

Tuscan White Bean Soup:

Ingredients:

1. 2 cans white beans, drained and rinsed
2. 4 cups vegetable broth
3. 1 onion, diced
4. 2 carrots, sliced
5. 2 stalks celery, diced
6. 3 cloves garlic, minced

7. 1 can diced tomatoes
8. 1 tsp dried rosemary
9. 1 tsp dried thyme
10. Salt and pepper to taste
11. Fresh parsley, chopped (for garnish)

Instructions:

1. In the crockpot, combine white beans, vegetable broth, diced onion, sliced carrots, diced celery, minced garlic, diced tomatoes, dried rosemary, dried thyme, salt, and pepper.
2. Stir well to combine the ingredients.
3. Cook on low for 6-8 hours or on high for 3-4 hours, until the vegetables are tender.
4. Adjust seasoning if needed.
5. Serve hot, garnished with fresh parsley.
6. Serve with crusty bread.

Prep Time: 15 minutes

Teriyaki Pork Tenderloin:

Ingredients:

1. 2 lbs pork tenderloin
2. 1/2 cup low-sodium soy sauce
3. 1/4 cup honey
4. 2 tbsp rice vinegar
5. 2 cloves garlic, minced
6. 1 tsp ginger, grated
7. 1/4 cup water
8. 1 tbsp cornstarch
9. Sesame seeds (for garnish)
10. Sliced green onions (for garnish)

Instructions:

1. Place pork tenderloin in the crockpot.
2. In a bowl, whisk together soy sauce, honey, rice vinegar, minced garlic, and grated ginger.
3. Pour the mixture over the pork, ensuring it's evenly coated.
4. Cook on low for 6-8 hours or on high for 3-4 hours, until pork is cooked through.
5. In a small bowl, mix water and cornstarch until smooth. Stir the mixture into the crockpot to thicken the sauce.

6. Shred the pork using two forks.
7. Serve hot, garnished with sesame seeds and sliced green onions.
8. Serve with rice or noodles.

Prep Time: 10 minutes

Sweet and Spicy Barbecue Ribs:

Ingredients:

1. 2 racks of baby back ribs
2. 1 cup barbecue sauce
3. 1/4 cup brown sugar
4. 2 tbsp Dijon mustard
5. 2 tbsp apple cider vinegar
6. 1 tsp smoked paprika
7. 1/2 tsp cayenne pepper (optional)
8. Salt and pepper to taste
9. Chopped fresh cilantro (for garnish)

Instructions:

1. Season the ribs with salt and pepper.
2. Place the ribs in the crockpot, standing them up against the sides.

3. In a bowl, whisk together barbecue sauce, brown sugar, Dijon mustard, apple cider vinegar, smoked paprika, cayenne pepper (if using), salt, and pepper.
4. Pour the sauce over the ribs, ensuring they are coated.
5. Cook on low for 6-8 hours or on high for 3-4 hours, until the meat is tender and falling off the bone.
6. Transfer the ribs to a baking sheet and brush them with additional barbecue sauce.
7. Broil for a few minutes until the sauce caramelizes.
8. Serve hot, garnished with chopped cilantro.

Prep Time: 15 minutes

Creamy Mushroom Risotto:

Ingredients:

1. 2 cups Arborio rice
2. 4 cups vegetable broth
3. 1 onion, diced
4. 8 oz mushrooms, sliced
5. 2 cloves garlic, minced
6. 1/2 cup grated Parmesan cheese
7. 1/4 cup heavy cream
8. 2 tbsp butter
9. 2 tbsp olive oil
10. Salt and pepper to taste
11. Chopped fresh parsley (for garnish)

Instructions:

1. In a pan, heat butter and olive oil over medium heat. Add diced onion and minced garlic. Sauté until onions are translucent.
2. Add sliced mushrooms and cook until golden.
3. Transfer the mushroom mixture to the crockpot.
4. Add Arborio rice and vegetable broth to the crockpot. Stir well to combine.
5. Cook on low for 2-3 hours, until the rice is tender and creamy.

6. Stir in grated Parmesan cheese and heavy cream.
7. Adjust seasoning with salt and pepper.
8. Serve hot, garnished with chopped parsley.

Prep Time: 15 minutes

Thai Peanut Chicken:

Ingredients:

1. 4 boneless, skinless chicken breasts
2. 1/2 cup peanut butter
3. 1/4 cup soy sauce
4. 2 tbsp honey
5. 2 tbsp lime juice
6. 2 cloves garlic, minced
7. 1 tsp ginger, grated
8. 1/4 cup water
9. 1 tbsp cornstarch
10. Chopped peanuts (for garnish)
11. Fresh cilantro, chopped (for garnish)

Instructions:

1. Place chicken breasts in the crockpot.
2. In a bowl, whisk together peanut butter, soy sauce, honey, lime juice, minced garlic, and grated ginger.
3. Pour the mixture over the chicken, ensuring it's evenly coated.
4. Cook on low for 4-6 hours or on high for 2-3 hours, until chicken is cooked through.
5. In a small bowl, mix water and cornstarch until smooth. Stir the mixture into the crockpot to thicken the sauce.
6. Shred the chicken using two forks.
7. Serve hot, garnished with chopped peanuts and fresh cilantro.
8. Serve with rice or noodles.

Prep Time: 10 minutes

Creamy Tomato Basil Soup:

Ingredients:

1. 1 can (28 oz) crushed tomatoes
2. 2 cups vegetable broth
3. 1 cup heavy cream
4. 1/4 cup tomato paste
5. 1 onion, diced
6. 2 cloves garlic, minced
7. 1/4 cup fresh basil leaves, chopped
8. Salt and pepper to taste
9. Grated Parmesan cheese (for garnish)
10. Fresh basil leaves (for garnish)

Instructions:

1. In the crockpot, combine crushed tomatoes, vegetable broth, heavy cream, tomato paste, diced onion, minced garlic, fresh basil leaves, salt, and pepper.
2. Stir well to combine the ingredients.
3. Cook on low for 4-6 hours or on high for 2-3 hours, until the flavors meld together.
4. Adjust seasoning if needed.
5. Serve hot, garnished with grated Parmesan cheese and fresh basil leaves.

6. Serve with crusty bread or grilled cheese sandwiches.

Prep Time: 10 minutes

Beef Stroganoff:

Ingredients:

1. 2 lbs beef stew meat, cubed
2. 1 onion, sliced
3. 8 oz mushrooms, sliced
4. 3 cloves garlic, minced
5. 1 cup beef broth
6. 1 cup sour cream
7. 2 tbsp Worcestershire sauce
8. 1 tbsp Dijon mustard
9. Salt and pepper to taste
10. Chopped fresh parsley (for garnish)

Instructions:

1. Place beef stew meat, sliced onion, sliced mushrooms, and minced garlic in the crockpot.
2. In a bowl, whisk together beef broth, sour cream, Worcestershire sauce, Dijon mustard, salt, and pepper.

3. Pour the mixture over the ingredients in the crockpot.
4. Cook on low for 6-8 hours or on high for 3-4 hours, until the beef is tender.
5. Adjust seasoning if needed.
6. Serve hot, garnished with chopped parsley.
7. Serve over egg noodles or rice.

Prep Time: 15 minutes

Vegetarian Chili:

Ingredients:

1. 2 cans kidney beans, drained and rinsed
2. 1 can black beans, drained and rinsed
3. 1 can diced tomatoes
4. 1 onion, diced
5. 2 bell peppers, diced
6. 2 cloves garlic, minced
7. 1 cup vegetable broth
8. 2 tbsp chili powder
9. 1 tsp cumin
10. 1/2 tsp paprika
11. Salt and pepper to taste
12. Chopped fresh cilantro (for garnish)

13. Sour cream (optional)

Instructions:

1. In the crockpot, combine kidney beans, black beans, diced tomatoes, diced onion, diced bell peppers, minced garlic, vegetable broth, chili powder, cumin, paprika, salt, and pepper.
2. Stir well to combine the ingredients.
3. Cook on low for 6-8 hours or on high for 3-4 hours, until the flavors meld together.
4. Adjust seasoning if needed.
5. Serve hot, garnished with chopped cilantro.
6. Add a dollop of sour cream if desired.
7. Serve with cornbread or tortilla chips.

Prep Time: 10 minutes

Lemon Garlic Chicken:

Ingredients:

1. 4 boneless, skinless chicken breasts
2. 1/4 cup lemon juice
3. 1/4 cup olive oil
4. 4 cloves garlic, minced
5. 1 tsp dried oregano
6. 1/2 tsp dried thyme
7. Salt and pepper to taste
8. Fresh parsley, chopped (for garnish)
9. Lemon slices (for garnish)

Instructions:

1. Place chicken breasts in the crockpot.
2. In a bowl, whisk together lemon juice, olive oil, minced garlic, dried oregano, dried thyme, salt, and pepper.
3. Pour the mixture over the chicken, ensuring it's evenly coated.
4. Cook on low for 4-6 hours or on high for 2-3 hours, until chicken is cooked through.
5. Serve hot, garnished with fresh parsley and lemon slices.
6. Serve with roasted vegetables or mashed potatoes.

Prep Time: 10 minutes

Mexican Quinoa:

Ingredients:

1. 1 cup quinoa, rinsed
2. 1 can black beans, drained and rinsed
3. 1 can diced tomatoes with green chilies
4. 1 cup frozen corn
5. 1 onion, diced
6. 2 cloves garlic, minced
7. 1 tsp chili powder
8. 1 tsp cumin
9. 1/2 tsp paprika
10. Salt and pepper to taste
11. Chopped fresh cilantro (for garnish)
12. Avocado slices (for garnish)

Instructions:

1. In the crockpot, combine quinoa, black beans, diced tomatoes with green chilies, frozen corn, diced onion, minced garlic, chili powder, cumin, paprika, salt, and pepper.
2. Stir well to combine the ingredients.

3. Cook on low for 2-3 hours, until the quinoa is cooked and the flavors meld together.
4. Adjust seasoning if needed.
5. Serve hot, garnished with chopped cilantro and avocado slices.
6. Serve as a main dish or as a side with tacos or grilled chicken.

Prep Time: 10 minutes

Chocolate Lava Cake:

Ingredients:

1. 1 cup all-purpose flour
2. 1/2 cup granulated sugar
3. 1/4 cup unsweetened cocoa powder
4. 1 tsp baking powder
5. 1/4 tsp salt
6. 1/2 cup milk
7. 2 tbsp unsalted butter, melted
8. 1 tsp vanilla extract
9. 1/2 cup semisweet chocolate chips
10. 3/4 cup hot water
11. Vanilla ice cream (for serving)

Instructions:

1. In a bowl, whisk together flour, sugar, cocoa powder, baking powder, and salt.
2. Stir in milk, melted butter, and vanilla extract until well combined.
3. Fold in chocolate chips.
4. Pour the batter into a greased crockpot.
5. In a separate bowl, mix hot water and additional sugar until dissolved.
6. Gently pour the sugar-water mixture over the batter in the crockpot.
7. Cook on low for 2-3 hours, until the cake is set around the edges but still gooey in the center.
8. Serve warm, topped with vanilla ice cream.

Prep Time: 10 minutes

CONCLUSION

As a result, "Crock Pot Cookbook for One: 30 Easy Delicious Recipes for Every Slow Cooking Meal" provides a wonderful selection of dishes created especially for cooking by yourself in the convenience of a crockpot. With this cookbook in your possession, you'll find a selection of delectable foods that are not only simple to make but also bursting with flavor.

This cookbook includes everything from substantial stews and cozy soups to tender meats and delicious desserts. These dishes meet your needs and offer filling meals for one, whether you're a busy professional, a student, or just someone who loves hassle-free cooking

Slow cooking has the advantage of enhancing tastes while requiring less time and work on your part. You may have a delectable, hot supper ready to eat when you get home with just a little preparation and the crockpot taking care of the rest. It's simple to follow along since each recipe includes step-by-step directions, ingredient lists, and estimated prep times.

With the help of the "Crock Pot Cookbook for One," you may improve your solo cooking skills and savor a range of delectable and wholesome meals without the hassle. Prepare to enjoy the speed, taste, and ease that slow cooking has to offer.

www.ingramcontent.com/pod-product-compliance
Lightning Source LLC
Chambersburg PA
CBHW070925141224
19003CB00030B/1106